The Magic Chain

Poems for Young Readers

Written and Illustrated by Elizabeth Uhlig

Marble House Editions

Published by Marble House Editions
96-09 66th Avenue (Suite 1D)
Rego Park, NY 11374
elizabeth.uhlig@yahoo.com
www.marble-house-editions.com

LCC Cataloguing-in-Publication Data

Uhlig, Elizabeth
The Magic Chain/by Elizabeth G. Uhlig
<u>Summary</u>: A Collection of Illustrated Poems for young Readers

ISBN 978-0-9834030-9-8

LCC Card Number 2015914092

Production Date: November, 2015

Plant & Location: Printed by Everbest Printing (Guangzhou,China), Co., Ltd
Job/Batch# 55512-0

In memory of Nelson

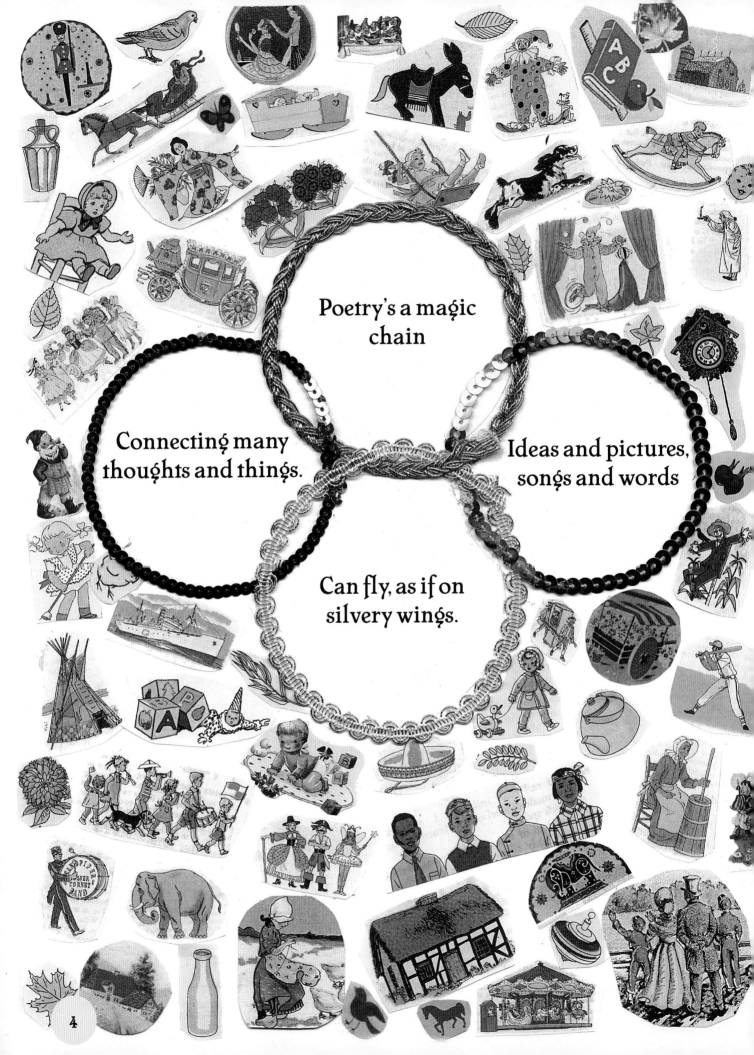

Poetry's a magic chain

Connecting many thoughts and things.

Ideas and pictures, songs and words

Can fly, as if on silvery wings.

4

Shall we ride the elephant?
If so, what will we see?
We will go adventuring,
Exploring, you and me.

Perhaps there'll be a lion,
Giraffes and zebras, too.
A panther and an antelope,
To only name a few.

From high up on the elephant
We'll see the open plain,
Pretend we've been to Africa,
And then go home again.

THE PATCHWORK HORSE

The Patchwork Horse that I made by myself
Sits with the other stuffed toys on the shelf.

He's all different colors 'cause he's made of soft rags,
and aprons and hankies and scraps of old flags.

Here he has polka dots, there he is plaid,
He's got stripes down the middle
But his eyes look so sad …

Perhaps it's because he is all made of patches
With so many patterns and nothing that matches.

Maybe he wishes he looked like the bear,
Who is only one color, or the cat over there,
With her fur that's so silky and shiny and pale,
Or the dog or the bunny I bought in a sale.

But the Patchwork Horse that I made by myself
Is the favorite of all my toys on the shelf.
I never would trade him, or leave him behind,
There's no other like him, he's one of a kind.

The Smallish Snowman

Last week we had a snowfall
So we went out to explore,
And made a smallish snowman
Who could stand outside our door.

Next day, when the sun came out
We thought he'd melt away,
So we put him in the freezer,
And there he had to stay.

9

But every time we took him out
He wasn't quite as twinkly,
His face was kind of shriveled
And was looking rather wrinkly.

We knew then that a snowman
Should be outside on the ground,
And if he melts, we'll build him back
Next time snow comes around.

Lullaby

Wind sighs low, its soft voice sweeping.
Moon's aglow, the world is sleeping.
Dreams enfold you as I hold you,
Nighttime's come, to sleep you go.

In Fairy Tales

In fairy tales what do we find?

Ideas to fascinate the mind.

Princesses locked up in towers,

Jewels that offer magic powers.

Charms and spells and beasts that speak,

Spooky castle doors that creak.

Palaces where royalty
Live as one big family.

Languages with
secret words,
Messages from
talking birds.

Folks dressed up in silk and lace,
Strolling 'round some fancy place.

Windows that look out on lands
Where seashells lie on shimmering sands.

Clever lads who masquerade,
and click and clack the flickering blade.

Darkened hallways, spiral stairs,
Cats that catch you unawares.

Puppets wearing costumes bright

that twinkle when they dance all night.

Servant girls who yearn to love
The princes they've been dreaming of.

And finally,
boys and girls
like you,

Who know that
none of this
is true.

Caribbean Lullaby

Milky stars, moon of glass,
See the slumbering lad and lass.
Summer night, warm and sweet
Moonbeams, moondreams sleepers meet.

Dulcet whispering of the sea,
Children sleeping 'neath a tree.
Falling blossom fragrant, white,
Gentle rhythms of the night.
Silky star, glassy moon,
Sing your sleepy little tune.

We Love the Earth

We love the Earth and all it has,
Everything that breathes and grows,
Take a closer look and see
The Earth is more than you'd suppose.

The Earth is meadows, hills and treetops,
Rivers, mountains, deserts, seas.
The Earth is cities, houses, rooftops,
And all kinds of families.

The Earth is quite a wondrous planet
Filled with things you don't know yet,
Places that you might discover,
People you have never met.

This chain is complete

until next we meet.